The
Interfaith
Prayer
Book

New Expanded Edition

Compiled by

TED BROWNSTEIN

LAKE WORTH INTERFAITH NETWORK

Ted Brownstein © 2001, 2014

Lake Worth Interfaith Network
1016 S. Lakeside Drive
Lake Worth, FL 33460
tedbro@aol.com

First edition 2001
Expanded second edition 2014

ISBN 978-0-9832609-7-4 (paperback)
ISBN 978-0-9832609-8-1 (eBook: Kindle / mobi)

Contents

"There can be no doubt whatever that the peoples of the world, of whatever race or religion, derive their inspiration from one heavenly Source and are subjects of one God."

∼ BAHÁ'Í FAITH

Ask and you will receive,
Knock and the door will be opened unto you.

∼ JESUS CHRIST

Foreword

This small prayer book is dedicated to the unity of all religions. The great faith traditions of mankind hold many of the same spiritual values: reverence for the Creator, appreciation of nature, respect for the sacredness of life, recognition of the need for personal and collective salvation and faith in divine governance over human affairs. Further, all promote the cultivation of virtues: love, kindness, honesty, humility, discipline and service.

Despite this foundation of shared beliefs, religious differences too often cause suspicion and animosity. Commonalities go unnoticed and misunderstanding prevails. The bridge to reconciliation is mutual understanding and respect. The more we know about other faiths, the more we shall see our commonalities.

Nothing reveals the heart of a people more than prayer. And sharing prayers from a variety of faith traditions has special potential. It can unite hearts in sacred acknowledgment of the mysteries of life and sacred values held in common.

Lead me from the unreal to the real,
Lead me from darkness to light,
Lead me from death to life,
From falsehood to truth.
Lead me from despair to hope,
From fear to trust.
Lead me from hate to love,
From war to peace.
Let peace fill our heart,
Our world, our universe.
Peace. Peace. Peace.

~ MOTHER TERESA, ADAPTED FROM UPANISHADS

Lake Worth
Interfaith Network

L ake Worth Interfaith Network (LWIN) is a group of individuals and faith-based communities dedicated to promoting acceptance and understanding among our diverse spiritual traditions through devotions, education and compassionate action.

LWIN hosts several annual events each year including a Thanksgiving Day Service of Gratitude, a World Aids Day Remembrance, a Martin Luther King Day Prayer Breakfast and a National Day of Prayer Gathering. Member faith communities take turns hosting. Programs consist of faith leaders taking turns sharing prayers, readings and music from their traditions. When we cannot find members from a particular faith tradition, prayers from the Interfaith Prayer Book can be read to create a representation of global spirituality.

LWIN members also arrange visitations to each other's houses of worship, building friendships and experiencing diverse prayer practices, ranging from the spirit-filled music of charismatic movements, to Maya fire ceremonies and the meditative silence of Quaker meetings. The positive comments received and resulting spiritual growth derived from these sharing encounters has been heartwarming.

LWIN hopes that sharing our experience will be helpful to other communities who desire to create similar local interfaith organizations. This publication of interfaith prayers is one step towards that end.

A final word should be said about the difficult task of deciding what selections and which faith traditions were to be included in this expanded version of the Interfaith Prayer Book. Recognizing that it would be beyond our scope and ability to represent every faith or denomination found in our ever shrinking planet, we chose to include those major faiths that had most influenced us, with particular attention to the groups that participate in our local, interfaith prayer gatherings. Sincerely, we ask pardon for those favorites, from any tradition, that were omitted and hope that this selection of worldwide prayers will inspire a deeper appreciation for the common worshipful impulse that is our universal human heritage.

Peace, Joy and Blessings,
Lake Worth Interfaith Network Board of Directors

Interfaith Gallery

Call to Prayer

Minarets from which Muslims
are called to public prayer.

Allah is most great. Allah is most great.
Allah is most great. Allah is most great.
I testify that there is no God except Allah.
I testify that there is no God except Allah.
I testify that Mohammad is the messenger of Allah.
I testify that Mohammad is the messenger of Allah.
Come to prayer! Come to prayer!
Come to success (in this life and the Hereafter)!
Come to success!
Allah is most great. Allah is most great.
There is no God except Allah.

~ Islam (Recited from the minarets
at times of public prayer)

Jewish women praying by the Western Wall, early 1900s

How goodly are your tents, O Jacob, your dwelling places, O Israel.
As for me, through Your abundant kindness I will enter Your House;
I will prostrate myself toward Your Holy Sanctuary in awe of You.
O God, I love the house wherein You dwell
And the place where Your glory resides.
I shall prostrate myself and bow,
I shall kneel before God, my Maker.
As for me, may my prayer to You, God,
Be at an opportune time;
O God, in Your abundant kindness,
Answer me with the truth of Your salvation.

~ JUDAISM (RECITED UPON ENTERING THE SYNAGOGUE)

12th century Rock-cut Church of Saint George in Africa.

I exhort therefore that, first of all, supplications, prayers,
intercessions and the giving of thanks, be made for all men;
for kings, and for all that are in authority; that we may lead a
quiet and peaceable life, in all goodness and honesty. For this
is acceptable in the sight of God our Savior.

~ CHRISTIANITY (NEW TESTAMENT)

Native African Prayer

OUR LORD, OUR MOON

May you be for us a moon of joy and happiness.
Let the young become strong
And the grown man retain his strength,
The pregnant woman be delivered
And the woman who has given birth suckle her child.
Let the stranger come to the end of his journey
And those who remain at home
Dwell safely in their houses.
Let the flocks that go to feed
In the pastures return happily.
May you be a moon of harvests and of calves.
May you be a moon of restoration and of good health.

~ MENSA TRIBE, ETHIOPIA

Prayer & Ritual in Traditional African Religion

When we speak of Africa in this context, we refer to Africa south of the Sahara desert. Even with this limitation, African Traditional Religion has proved to be very difficult to define. There is no single simple all-encompassing definition. A broad diversity exists between East, West and South Africa. Unfortunately, some scholars have misunderstood African Religion, defining it with misleading terms such as animism, fetishism, magic, superstitions, primitive religion, ancestor worship, paganism, etc.

The difficulty in defining African traditional religion arises from the fact that it is lived rather than preached or taught. Dogmas and doctrines are non-existent. There are no sacred books. Whoever would like to observe or study it has to do it in practical life. Its "sacred texts" are found in rituals, ceremonies and festivals; shrines, sacred places and religious objects; art and symbols; music and dance; proverbs, riddles and wise sayings; names of people and places; myths and legends; beliefs and customs.

African religion is tribal and clan based. Therefore, it may be said that each group retains its own distinct form, comparable to the differences between denominations in Christianity with common essential beliefs about the Supreme Being, nature, life, death, and life after death, etc. These similarities are more important than the differences.

Prayer practice has been influenced by exposure for many centuries to Islam and Christianity. Most Africans prayers show the influence of both traditional and imported forms.

~ Abridgment of words of Father Richard Nnyombi

Native American Prayer

Harmony with nature is a predominant theme in many native traditions, ranging through North, Central and South America. The world is structured according to the four cardinal compass points, east, west, north and south, and by the vertical axis linking mother earth below with father sky above. All of creation, mountains and plains, plants and fruits, animals and humans are seen as interconnected sacred elements. The well-being of each is dependent upon the whole.

PRAYER TO FOUR CARDINAL DIRECTIONS

Great Spirit of Light, come to me out of the East (red) with the power of the rising sun. Let there be light in my words, let there be light on my path that I walk. Let me remember always that you give the gift of a new day. And never let me be burdened with sorrow by not starting over again.

Great Spirit of Love, come to me with the power of the North (white). Make me courageous when the cold wind falls upon me. Give me strength and endurance for everything that is harsh, everything that hurts, everything that makes me squint. Let me move through life ready to take what comes from the north.

Great Life-Giving Spirit, I face the West (black), the direction of sundown. Let me remember everyday that the moment will come when my sun will go down. Never let me forget that I must fade into you. Give me a beautiful color, give me a great sky for setting, so that when it is my time to meet you, I can come with glory.

Great Spirit of Creation, send me the warm and soothing winds from the South (yellow). Comfort me and caress me when I am tired and cold. Unfold me like the gentle breezes that unfold the leaves on the trees. As you give to all the earth your warm, moving wind, give to me, so that I may grow close to you in warmth. Man did not create the web of life, he is but a strand in it. Whatever man does to the web, he does to himself.

～ CHIEF SEATTLE, DUWAMISH TRIBE

SIX DIRECTIONS OF AID

Oh our Father, the Sky, hear us and make us strong.
Oh our Mother the Earth, hear us and give us support.
Oh Spirit of the East, send us your wisdom.
Oh Spirit of the South, may we tread your path of life.
Oh Spirit of the West, may we always be ready for the long
    journey.
Oh Spirit of the North, purify us with your cleansing winds.

~ LAKOTA, SOUTH DAKOTA

LIFE AND DEATH

GRANDMOTHER East: From you comes the sun which brings
life to us all; I ask that you have the sun shine on my friends
here, and bring a new life to them—a life without the pain
and sadness of the world; and to their families, bring your sun
for they also need your light for their lives.

GRANDFATHER South: You bring the storms from the south
which brings the rains to nourish us and our crops. Be gentle
when you fall on my friends; and as the rain touches them, let
it wash away the pain and sadness that they carry with them.

GRANDMOTHER West: You take the sun from us and cradle it
in your arms, then you bring darkness onto us so that we may
sleep. When you bring the darkness to my friends here, do so
without the nightmares that we have had for so long. Let your
stars and moon shine on my friends in a gentle manner; and
as they look at the stars, they remember that those stars are
the spirits of my friends shining on them and those friends are
at peace.

GRANDFATHER North: You are the Warrior, you have ridden
alongside my friends here into battle, you have also felt their
love and caring when you were wounded or lonely; ride
alongside of them, for now they are in this the hardest battle

for their lives, the battle for inner peace. Now is the time for you to care for them.

GRANDFATHER Sky: May your songs of the winds and clouds sweep the pain and sadness out of my friends' hearts; as they hear those songs, let them know the peace of the songs of peace.

GRANDMOTHER Earth: I have asked all the other GrandFathers and GrandMothers to help my friends rid themselves of the troubles that weigh so heavy on their hearts. This way, the weight they carry will be less; and they will walk more softly on you.

GRANDMOTHER Earth, from your womb all spirits have come when they return to you; cradle them gently in your arms and allow them to join their friends in the skies. If they want to hurry themselves to you, tell them you are not ready; and they must wait, for now they can pass on peace to others.

∿ LAKOTA, DEDICATED TO
THE DEAD FROM THE VIETNAM WAR

Medicine Wheel, Big Horn National Forest, Wyoming

LET US BE HAPPY ON EARTH

Oh Great Spirit, Creator of all things;
Human beings, trees, grass, berries.
Help us, be kind to us.
Let us be happy on earth.
Let us lead our children
To a good life and old age.
These our people; give them good minds
To love one another.
Oh Great Spirit,
Be kind to us,
Give these people the favor
To see green trees,
Green grass, flowers and berries
This next spring;
So we all meet again.
Oh Great Spirit,
We ask of you.

~ MOHAWK, NEW YORK

LOOK AT OUR BROKENNESS

Grandfather, look at our brokenness.
We know that in all creation
Only the human family
Has strayed from the Sacred Way.

We know that we are the ones
Who are divided And we are the ones
Who must come back together
To walk in the Sacred Way.

Grandfather, Sacred One,
Teach us love, compassion and honor
That we may heal the earth
And heal each other.

~ OJIBWA, ONTARIO

MAY IT BE BEAUTIFUL ALL AROUND ME

House made of dawn.
House made of evening light.
House made of dark cloud.
House made of grasshoppers.

Dark cloud is at the door.
The zigzag lightning stands high upon it.
An offering I make.
Restore my feet for me.
Restore my legs for me.
Restore my body for me.
Restore my mind for me.
Restore my voice for me.

Happily I recover.
Happily my interior becomes cool.
Happily I go forth.
My interior feeling cool, may I walk.
No longer sore, may I walk.
Impervious to pain, may I walk.
With lively feelings may I walk.
As it used to be long ago, may I walk.

Happily may I walk.
Happily, with abundant dark clouds, may I walk.
Happily, with abundant showers, may I walk.
Happily, with abundant plants, may I walk.
Happily, on a trail of pollen, may I walk.
Happily may I walk.
Being as it used to be long ago, may I walk.

May it be beautiful before me.
May it be beautiful behind me.
May it be beautiful below me.
May it be beautiful above me.
May it be beautiful all around me.

~ NAVAJO, ARIZONA

MAKER OF THE TREES

May all I say and all I think
Be in harmony with thee,
God within me, God beyond me,
Maker of the trees.

In me be the windswept truth of shore pine,
Fragrance of balsam and spruce,
The grace of hemlock.
In me the truth of douglas fir, straight and tall,
Strong-trunked land hero of fireproof bark,
Sheltering tree of life, cedar's truth be mine,
Cypress truth, juniper aroma, strength of yew.

May all I say and all I think
Be in harmony with thee,
God within me, God beyond me,
Maker of the trees.

In me be the truth of stream-lover willow
Soil-giving alder
Hazel of sweet nuts,
Wisdom-branching oak.
In me the joy of crabapple, great maple, vine maple,
Cleansing cascara and lovely dogwood.
And the gracious truth of copper branched arbutus,
Bright with color and fragrance,
Be with me on Earth.
May all I say and all I think
Be in harmony with thee,
God within me, God beyond me,
Maker of the trees.

~ CHINOOK, OREGON

Value of Religion

Trouble no one about their religion; respect others in their views, and demand that they respect yours. Love your life, perfect your life, beautify all things in your life. Seek to make your life long and of service to your people. Always give a word or sign of salute when meeting or passing a stranger if in a lonely place. Show respect to all people, but grovel to none. When you arise in the morning, give thanks for the light, for your life and strength. Give thanks for your food and for the joy of living. If you see no reason for giving thanks, the fault lies in yourself.

∿ SHAWNEE, CHIEF TECUMSEH, NORTH AMERICA

The message of our grandparents is that since the creation of Light each person has spiritual capacity to understand the hidden powers of the cosmos. To capture the messages which Nature has for us, all are invited to have an open mind which is receptive and willing to embrace the energy of change. This spiritual state of preparation empowers all willing walkers to follow the new cycle of life which began with the advent of the Fifth Sun in December 2012. In the riches of rebirth, a new dawn ushers in an era of liberation and global healing, the sacred fire of the "yo internal" is rekindled, the cosmic umbilical cord is reestablished connecting us to the future and the past, facilitating human transformation and growth.

∿ MAYA, MIGUEL ANGEL CHINQUIN YAT, CENTRAL AMERICA

The real value of the practices of the Andean sacred tradition is to help us to live life consciously. To live life consciously. It is not only about cultivation qualities that enhance well-being, such as non-judgment, unconditional love, forgiveness, patience and the like. It is also about being conscious of your every action, thought, feeling, emotion, intention, intuition, dream and vision. It is about bridging worlds, not being immersed in either the mundane or the magical.

∿ ANDEAN SCHOLAR, JOAN PARISI
WILCOX, SOUTH AMERICA

NOW IT IS THE WOMAN
WHO HAS THE TORCH

Oh, Powerful Lady
Oh, Lady of the Flame
Oh, Lady of the Two Worlds
Oh, Lady, well beloved of the Father
Arise now to balance the Male Divine Warrior
To bring the Female Power of Peace
Oh, Ix Chel, Blessed Moon Mother
You are the Forever Feminine, as above so below
From all eternity, you are the primordial force that nurtures
the astral and the physical worlds. Oh, Lady, bring us peace.
Oh, Powerful Lady, bring us peace.

~ MAYA PRAYER FOR THE ADVENT OF
THE ENERGY OF QUINTO SOL

READING OF POPUL VUH

Make my guilt vanish,
Heart of Sky, Heart of Earth;
Grant me a favor,
Give me strength, give me courage
In my heart, in my head,
Since you are my mountain and my plain;
May there be no falsehood and no stain,
And may this reading of the Popol Vuh
Come out clear as dawn,
And may the sifting of ancient times
Be complete in my heart, in my head;
And make my guilt vanish,
My grandmothers, grandfathers,
And however many souls of the dead there may be,
You who speak with the Heart of Sky and Earth,
May all of you together give strength
To the reading I have undertaken.

⁓ MAYA PRAYER FOR VISITATION TO SACRED SITES AND
READING THE CREATION EPIC, POPUL VUH.

Tikal Main Pyramid, Guatemala

CREATING SACRED SPACE

South

To the Spirits of the South

Great Serpent, Sachamama, Amaru

Wrap your golden coils of healing light around us.

Teach us to release our past the way you shed your skin, all at once.

Teach us to walk with beauty and grace on the belly of Mother Earth.

Teach us that beauty is always in us, around us, and surrounding us.

Teach us the beauty path.

West

To the Spirits of the West

Mother Sister Jaguar, Otorongo

Protect this medicine space.

Show us the path inwards to our own inner mastery

Where we radiate the unconditional love of our heart.

Teach us the way of peace and integrity.

North

To the spirits of the North Hummingbird, Ciraq Kenti,

Spirits of the land, Guardians of the land

Ancient ones

Help us remember ancient wisdom, ancient knowledge and to drink deeply from the well of immortality

Whisper to us in the wind—in the crackle of the fire—in the sacred space of our heart

We are thankful and grateful to you who have come before us and after us

Teach us to walk the sacred path.

East

To the spirits of the East Eagle, Condor

Thank you for kicking us out of the nest so we would learn to
grow our own wings

Take us to higher grounds and illuminate our destiny You who are
the great visionary

Teach us to always see through the eyes of our heart.

Earth

Mother Earth, Pachamama, Tierra Madre

We celebrate all those that live within you, around you, and
surrounding you

All of our relations

We thank you for sustaining us in all of our lifetimes

Sing to us, our original healed soul song

Teach us to remember who we are.

Heaven

Father Sun, Inti Taita Chaska,

Inka messenger to the star people

Hold us in between the tick and the tock, between the spaces

Hold us in the place of infinity

Where all the stories exist simultaneously

Where all the healing happens instantaneously

Thank you for bringing us together

For letting us sing our soul songs, one more day in one more way

Teach us that we are the ones we have been waiting for.

$\sim$ INCA

Machu Picchu, Peru

Jewish Prayer

Artist's conception of ancient Jerusalem with the Temple in the foreground.

Traditional Jewish practice calls for the recitation of specific prayers three times a day, morning, noon and evening. Included are the Shema which proclaims the Oneness of God and selected Psalms.

THE SHEMA

Hear, O Israel: The Lord our God is one Lord:

Blessed is His name, whose glorious kingdom is forever and ever.

And thou shalt love the Lord thy God with all thine heart, and with all thy soul, and with all thy might.

And these words, which I command thee this day, shall be in thine heart:

And thou shalt teach them diligently unto thy children, and shalt talk of them when thou sittest in thine house, and when thou walkest by the way, and when thou liest down, and when thou risest up.

And thou shalt bind them for a sign upon thine hand, and they shall be as frontlets between thine eyes.

And thou shalt write them upon the posts of thy house, and on thy gates.

שְׁמַע | יִשְׂרָאֵל, יהוה | אֱלֹהֵינוּ, יהוה | אֶחָד

Sh'ma Yisrael Adonai Elohaynu Adonai Echad.

Notes: The Shema is the most central prayer of Jewish life. It invokes the sacred name of God, and acknowledges His oneness, the hallmark of monotheism. The Shema is recited each evening and morning according to the saying, "when you lie down and when you get up." Phylacteries, which are leather straps holding small cases of scripture, are tied onto the arms and forehead according to the saying, "and thou shall bind them for a sign upon thine hand and . . . as frontlets between thine eyes." These same verses are posted on the doorposts of Jewish homes in the *mezuzah* according to the saying, "thou shall write them upon the posts of thy house."

This prayer is quoted almost exactly from Deuteronomy 6:4–9, except for the second line, "Blessed . . . ever." This line has a mystical origin. Tradition says that when Moses ascended Mount Sinai to receive the Ten Commandments, he heard the angels around the divine throne saying this line repeatedly. It is said quietly so that the angels don't know that their most important prayer was stolen. However, on Yom Kippur it is recited out loud, so desperate is the need for salvation.

HALLEL—PSALMS OF PRAISE

Praise ye the LORD.

Praise ye the LORD from the heavens: praise him in the heights.

Praise ye him, all his angels: praise ye him, all his hosts.

Praise ye him, sun and moon: praise him, all ye stars of light.

Praise him, ye heavens of heavens, and ye waters that be above the heavens.

Let them praise the name of the LORD: for he commanded, and they
were created.

He hath also established them for ever and ever:

He hath made a decree which shall not pass.

Praise the LORD from the earth, ye dragons, and all deeps:

Fire, and hail; snow, and vapours; stormy wind fulfilling his word:

Mountains, and all hills; fruitful trees, and all cedars:

Beasts, and all cattle; creeping things, and flying fowl:

Kings of the earth, and all people; princes, and all judges of the earth:

Both young men, and maidens; old men, and children:

Let them praise the name of the LORD:

For his name alone is excellent; his glory is above the earth and heaven.

He also exalteth the horn of his people, the praise of all his saints;

Even of the children of Israel, a people near unto him.

Praise ye the LORD.

~ PSALM 148

As for me, my tongue shall praise Thy righteousness . . .

Thou has placed on my lips a fountain of praise

And in my heart the secrets of the origin of all human works

And the understanding of the perfect way

And judgments concerning all deeds done by men.

You judge the man of justice by Thy truth

And condemn the wicked for their guilt.

You announce peace to all men of the Covenant

And utter a dreadful cry of woe for all those who breach it.

May they bless all Thy works always.

Blessed be thy name for ever and ever. Amen. Amen.

~ SONGS OF THE SAGES, DEAD SEA SCROLLS

Hallelujah.
Praise, O ye servants of the LORD,
Praise the name of the LORD.
Blessed be the name of the LORD
From this time forth and for ever.
From the rising of the sun to the going down thereof
The Lord's name is to be praised.
The Lord is high above all nations,
His glory is above the heavens.
Who is like the LORD our God,
That is enthroned on high,
That looketh down low
Upon heaven and upon the earth?
Who raiseth up the poor out of the dust,
And lifteth up the needy out of the dunghill;
That He may set him with princes,
Even with the princes of his people.
Who maketh the barren woman to dwell in her house
As a joyful mother of children.
Hallelujah.

$\sim$ PSALM 113

When Israel went from Egypt,
The house of Jacob from a people of foreign language;
Judah was his sanctuary, and Israel his dominion.
The sea saw it, and fled; the Jordan was driven back.
The mountains skipped like rams, and the hills like lambs.
What ails you, O sea, that you flee?
O Jordan, that you are driven back?
O mountains, that you skip like rams?
And you O hills, like lambs?
Tremble, earth, at the presence of the Lord,
At the presence of the God of Jacob;
Who turned the rock into a pool of water,
The flint into a fountain of waters.

$\sim$ PSALM 114

TIKUN OLAM

The Hebrew phrase tikun olam means "healing the world." A central belief of Judaism is that each generation must pray and work in partnership with God towards universal harmony and peace.

Peace to you, ministering angels, messengers of the Most High,
    from the King of kings, the Holy One, blessed be He.
Enter in peace, angels of peace, messengers of the Most High,
    from the King of kings, the Holy One, blessed be He.
Bless me with peace, angels of peace, messengers of the Most
    High, from the King of kings, the Holy One, blessed be He.
Depart in peace, angels of peace, messengers of the Most High,
    from the King of kings, the Holy One, blessed be He.

                ～ 17TH CENTURY SABBATH PRAYER

May the one who causes peace to reign upon the heavens, let
    peace reign upon Israel and upon all the peoples of the world,
    and we say, amen.

                ～ OSEH SHALOM

Come let us go up to the mountain of the Lord,
    that we may walk the paths of the Most High.
And we shall beat our swords into plowshares
    and our spears into pruning hooks.
Nation shall not lift up sword against nation—
    neither shall they learn war any more.

                ～ ISAIAH

A Jewish View of Prayer

Prayer: Its Hebrew name is, *tefillah*, a word that gives us an insight into the Torah's concept of prayer. The root of *tefillah* means to *judge*, to *differentiate*, to *clarify*, to *decide*. In life, we constantly sort out evidence from rumor, valid options from wild speculations, fact from fancy. Thus, prayer is the soul's yearning to define what truly matters and to ignore the trivialities that often masquerade as essential

~ Siddur Avodas HaLev

God knows our requirements without being reminded. He knows them better than we do. If prayer were intended only to inform God of our desires and deficiencies, it would be unnecessary. Its true purpose is to raise the level of the supplicants by helping them develop true perceptions of life so that they can become worthy of His blessing.

This is the function of the evaluating, decision-making process of prayer. The Hebrew word for prayer is reflexive, indicating that the one who prays acts upon himself. Prayer is a process of self-evaluation, *self*-judgment; a process of removing oneself from the *tumult* of life to a little corner of truth and refastening the bonds that tie one to the *purpose* of life.

~ The Complete Artscroll Siddur

Hindu Prayer

Hindu Tower Temple in Tamilnadu, India

According to Hindu theology, among the many thousands of names of God, no name suits God, who abides in the heart, devoid of thought, so truly, aptly, and beautifully as the name "I am." Of all the known names of God, the name of God "I am" alone will resound triumphantly when the ego is destroyed, rising as the silent supreme word in the heart-space.

Be Pleased to Show Mercy, O God

Thou art the Imperishable, the supreme Object of Knowledge;
Thou art the ultimate resting-place of this universe;
Thou art the immortal guardian of the eternal right,
Thou art the everlasting Spirit, I hold.
Without beginning, middle, or end, of infinite power,
    Of infinite arms, whose eyes are the moon and sun,
I see Thee, whose face is flaming fire,
Burning this whole universe with Thy radiance.
For this region between heaven and earth
Is pervaded by Thee alone, and all the directions;
Seeing this Thy wondrous, terrible form,
The triple world trembles, O exalted one!
Homage be to Thee from in front and from behind,
Homage be to Thee from all sides, Thou All!
O Thou of infinite might, Thy prowess is unmeasured;
Thou attainest all; therefore Thou art All!
Thou art the Father of the world of things that
    move and move not,
And Thou art its revered, most venerable Guru;
There is no other like Thee-how then a greater?
Even, in the three worlds,
    O Thou of matchless greatness
Therefore, bowing and prostrating my body,
I beg grace of Thee, the Lord to be revered:
As a father to his son, as a friend to his friend,
As a lover to his beloved, be pleased to show mercy, O God!

                  ~ FROM THE BHAGAVAD-GITA, XI

Nonviolence is the law of our species as violence is
   the law of the brute.
The spirit lies dormant in the brute,
   and he knows no law but that of physical might.
The dignity of man requires obedience to a higher law—
   to the strength of the spirit.

   ∼ MAHATMA GANDHI

PEACE PRAYERS

I desire neither earthly kingdom, nor even freedom
   from birth and death.
I desire only the deliverance from grief of all those afflicted by
   misery.
Oh Lord, lead us from the unreal to the real from darkness to
   light from death to immortality.
May there be peace in celestial regions.
May there be peace on earth.
May the waters be appeasing.
May herbs be wholesome and may trees and plants bring
   peace to all.
May all beneficent beings bring peace to us.
May thy wisdom spread peace all through the world.
May all things be a source of peace to all and to me.
Om Shanti, Shanti, Shanti (Peace, Peace, Peace).
O Krishna, Lord of Yoga! Surely blessing, and victory, and
   power shall not fail for Thy most mighty sake.

   ∼ BHAGAVAD-GITA, XVIII

A Hindu View of Prayer

The kitten mews and the mother cat runs and carries it away. Even so, the devotee cries and the Lord comes to his rescue. Prayer is nearness to God. It is tuning one's mind with the mind of God. It is focusing the thoughts on God and meditating on Him. Prayer is surrendering oneself to God completely, and melting the mind and ego in silence, in God. Prayer represents a mystic state when the individual consciousness is absorbed in God. It is an uplifting of the soul to God, an act of love and adoration to Him. It is worship and glorification of God. It is thanksgiving to God for all His blessings.

Whose prayer is heard? Prayer should spring from the heart and should not be mere lip-homage. Empty prayer is like sounding brass or tinkling cymbal. Prayer that comes from a sincere, pure heart is at once heard by the Lord. The prayer of a cunning, crooked, wicked man is never heard.

Breath has been given to you by the Lord to be spent in prayer. There are no problems that cannot be solved by prayer, no suffering that cannot be allayed by prayer, no difficulties that cannot be surmounted by prayer, and no evil that cannot be overcome by prayer. Prayer is the miracle by which God's power flows into human veins. Therefore kneel down and pray. When the storms of lust and anger, vanity and viciousness rage within your bosom, kneel down and pray. For the Lord, and He alone, has the power over the elements. In thy supplication is thy strength, shielded by His mercy, and spurred on the path of righteousness by His Divine Will.

∽ Swami Paramananda

Zoroastrian Prayer

Parsi (Zoroastrian) Fire Temple, Mumbai, India

Founded by Zarathustra, Zoroatrianism is the pre-Islamic faith of Persia (Iran), where God is known by the name Ahura Mazda, meaning Illuminating Wisdom. Due to persecution in the cradle of its birth, most Zoroastrians fled to India where the greatest number now live. The writings of Zarathustra are found in the Avestas which depict the world as a great battleground between good and evil. Zoroastrian prayer focuses on the inner life of the worshipper, emphasizing good thought as a prerequisite for good deeds.

UNIVERSAL WELLBEING

I pray for the entire creation,
And for the generation which is now alive
And for that which is just coming into life
And for that which shall come thereafter.
I pray for that sanctity which leads to well-being
Which has long afforded shelter
Which goes on hand in hand with it
Which joins it in its walk
And of itself becoming its close companion
As it delivers forth its bidding,
Bearing every form of healing virtue which comes to us.
And so may we be blessed with the greatest,
And the best,
And most beautiful benefits of sanctity.
Aidun bad—so may it be.

∼ MORNING PRAYER FROM AVESTA YASNA 52:1-3

TWO PATHS

Every good thought, every good word,
Every good deed is of wisdom born.
Every evil thought, every evil word,
Every evil deed is not of wisdom born.
Every good thought, every good word, every good deed
     Leads to the best existence.
Every evil thought, every evil word, every evil deed
     Leads to the worst life.
Every good thought, every good word, every good deed
     Is the best existence.
That which is begotten of righteous order
The one path is that of *Asha* (the ideal plane of existence).
All others are not-paths.

∼ AVESTA YASNA 72:10-11

An End to Violence

O Ahura Mazda,
Let good rulers rule us, not evil rulers,
With the actions of the Good, O Piety!
Perfect thou for man, O thou Most Good,
The future birth, and for the cow skilled husbandry.
Let her grow fat for our nourishing.
Give us peaceful dwelling,
Give us lasting life and strength, the beloved of Good Thought.
For Mazda Ahura made the plants to grow
At the time of the birth of the First Life.
Violence must be put down!
Against cruelty make a stand,
You who would make sure of the reward of Good Thought,
To whose company the holy man belongs.
His dwelling place shall be in thy House, O Ahura.

∾ Avesta Yasna 48:5-7

Triumph of Peace

May peace triumph over discord here,
Generous giving over avarice,
Reverence over contempt,
Speech with truthful words over lying utterance.
May the Righteous Order gain the victory.

∾ Avesta Yasna 60:5

Ancient Zoroastrian symbol depicting a man emerging from a winged disk. A variety of interpretations have been offered. One of the most common explains it as the human soul soaring in the heavens riding upon the glory of the sun.

Happiness

O Maker of the material world, thou Holy One!
Which is the first place where the earth feels most happy?
Ahura Mazda answered: 'It is the place whereon one of the faithful
    steps forward
O Maker of the material world, thou Holy One!
Which is the second place where the earth feels most happy?
Ahura Mazda answered: 'It is the place whereon one of the faithful
    erects a house
With a priest within, with cattle, with a wife, with children,
And good herds within;
Where the cattle continue to thrive,
Virtue to thrive, fodder to thrive, the dog to thrive,
The wife to thrive, the child to thrive, the fire to thrive,
And every blessing of life to thrive.

                  ~ Avesta Vendidad 1–3

May God give happiness
To the person who gives happiness to others.
I pray for power and courage
To defend the good.
O God, grant me peace and blessings.

                  ~ Gatha Song

Give me, O fire of Ahura Mazda,
The best of the world of righteousness,
The shining, the All-Happy,
So that I may gain good reward and happiness in my soul.

                  ~ Avesta, Atash Niyayesh 12

SALVATION OF THE WICKED

Praise be to the merciful Lord
Who bestows rewards for meritorious deeds
On those who obey his commands according to his will,
And at last will liberate even the wicked from (the torture of) hell
And will embellish with purity the whole creation.

～ AVESTA, NAM STAYISHN 7

THE STRUGGLE BETWEEN GOOD AND EVIL

The Maker of the evil world, Angra Mainyu, said to Zarathustra: 'Do not destroy my creatures, O holy Zarathustra! Thou art the son of Pourushaspa; by thy mother I was invoked. Renounce the good Religion of the worshippers of Mazda, and thou shalt gain such a great boon and become ruler of the nations.'

Zarathustra said in answer: 'No! never will I renounce the good Religion of the worshippers of Mazda, either for body or life, though they should tear away the breath!'

Again to him said the Maker of the evil world, Angra Mainyu: 'By whose Word wilt thou strike, by whose Word wilt thou repel, by whose weapon will the good creatures (strike and repel) my creation?'

Zarathustra said in answer: 'The Word taught by Mazda, this is my weapon, my best weapon! By this Word will I strike, by this Word will I repel, by this weapon will the good creatures (strike and repel thee), O evil-doer, Angra Mainyu!

The Good Spirit made the creation; he made it in the boundless time. He is the good, the wise Sovereign.'

～ AVESTA VENDIDAD 6–9

Zarathustra and the Avestas

Zarathustra was the founder of Zoroastrianism. Some view him as a prophet and others as a spiritual philosopher. His dialogues and hymns are recorded in the Avestas. He broke with the customary belief of his Age that religion was determined by one's tribe or family. Each individual became responsible to seek truth independently. In the after-life each individual would be rewarded or punished according to his or her personal deeds, good or evil.

Little is known of Zarathustra's personal life. Scholarly opinion places him sometime between the sixth and tenth centuries before Christ. Cyrus the Great, the Persian conqueror of Babylon of the sixth century BCE, is known to have been a Zoroastrian.

Zoroastrian View of Prayer

For Zoroastrians, individual prayer is a defining feature of their religiosity. Daily prayers are seen as imparting spiritual strength and resistance against harm and ill health. Praying throughout the day can be seen as an opportunity to take a periodic recess from the pressures of work to develop a quiet space and a calm mind to recite a *manthra* and meditate.

Orthodox Zoroastrians pray five times per day, at sunrise, noon, mid-afternoon, sunset and midnight. Turning toward a source of light is preferred when praying. Natural light is best. For the morning prayers they will face the rising sun (or east) and for their evening prayers they will face the setting sun (or west) while reciting their *manthra*. At night, they will, if possible, light a wood burning fire in a censer, a flame in a vegetable oil lamp or a candle. The censer or lamp can be part of a home altar.

Prayer time is sacred time which is set apart from other activities of the day by ritual preparation called *padyap* (washing face and limbs accompanied by oils and incense) and when possible by donning special clothing, a head covering and a white vest with a cord wrapped around the waist.

Buddhist Prayer

Buddhist Gateway at Sanchi, India

The purpose of Buddhist prayer and meditation is to purify the thoughts. By focusing one's attention on what is pure and holy, simple and free from passion, one grows in happiness and attains enlightenment. This is suggested in the opening verses of the Dhammapada:

> What we are is the result of what we have thought, is built by our thoughts, is made up of our thoughts.
> If one speaks or acts with an impure thought, suffering follows one, like the wheel of the cart follows the foot of the ox.
> What we are is the result of what we have thought, is built by our thoughts, is made up of our thoughts.
> If one speaks or acts with a pure thought, happiness follows one, like a shadow that never leaves.

Meditation quiets the mind. By focusing on a single sound or idea, troubling thoughts are set aside and peace enters. Mantra meditation is chanting meditation. One sits quietly and repeats certain sacred words or phrases. The goal is to reach a higher state of consciousness and spiritual ecstasy. Perhaps the most famous mantra in Tibetan Buddhism is OM MANI PADME HUM which can be translated as "the jewel in the heart of the lotus."

Om Mani Padme Hum (in Tibetan Characters)

DETACHMENT

It is good to control the mind,
    which is difficult to restrain, fickle, and wandering.
A tamed mind brings happiness.
Let the wise guard their thoughts,
    which are difficult to perceive, tricky, and wandering.
Thoughts well guarded bring happiness.
Those who restrain their mind,
    which travels far alone without a body, hiding in a cave, will
    be free from the restrictions of death.
If a person's mind is unsteady,
    if it does not know the true path,
    if one's peace of mind is troubled,
    wisdom is not perfected.
There is no fear for the one whose thought is untroubled,
    whose mind is not confused,
    who has ceased to think of good and bad,
    who is aware.

~ DHAMMAPADA, 3. THOUGHT

THE ONE
I CALL HOLY

The sun shines by day; the moon lights up the night;
    the warriors shine in their armor;
    the holy one shines in meditation;
    but the awakened shines radiantly all day and night. . .
No one should hurt a holy one,
    but no holy one should strike back.
Woe to the one who hurts a holy one;
    more woe to the one who strikes back.
I do not call one holy because of one's family or mother.
If one has property, one is called superior.
The one I call holy is free of property and all attachment.
The one I call holy has cut all chains, never trembles,
    has passed beyond attachments and is independent.
The one I call holy has cut the strap, the thong,
    and the chain with all their encumbrances,
    has removed the bar and is awakened.
The one I call holy, though having committed no offense,
    patiently bears reproach, ill-treatment, and imprisonment, has
    endurance for one's force and strength for one's army.
The one I call holy has let go of anger, hate, pride, and hypocrisy,
    like a mustard seed falls from the point of a needle.
The one I call holy speaks true words
    that are useful and not harsh so that no one is offended. . .

                ~ DHAMMAPADA, 26. THE HOLY ONE

THE REFUGE CHANT

At the foot of the Bodhi tree, beautifully seated, peaceful and
smiling, the living source of understanding and compassion,
to the Buddha I go for refuge.

(bell)

The path of mindful living, leading to healing, joy and
enlightenment, the way of peace, to the Dharma I go for refuge.

(bell)

The loving and supporting community of practice, realizing
harmony, awareness, and liberation, to the Sangha I go for
refuge.

(bell)

I vow to practice mindful breathing and smiling,
looking deeply into things.
I vow to understand living beings and their suffering,
to cultivate compassion and loving kindness,
and to practice joy and equanimity.

(bell)

I vow to offer joy to one person in the morning
and to help relieve the grief of one person in the afternoon.
I vow to live simply and sanely, content with just a few
possessions. . .
I vow to let go of all worries and anxiety in order to be light and
free.

(bell)

I am aware that I owe much to my parents,
teachers, friends and all beings.
I vow to be worthy of their trust, to practice wholeheartedly,
so that understanding and compassion will flower,
and I can help living beings be free from their suffering.
May the Buddha, the Dharma, and the Sangha support my efforts.

(three sounds of the bell)

HAPPINESS

Whatsoever beings are here assembled,
Those of the earth or those of the air,
May all of them be happy!
Let them all listen attentively to my words!

Listen here, all beings!
Show your love to those humans
Who, day and night, bring offerings to you.
Therefore, guard them diligently.

Whatever treasure there be,
Either here or in the world beyond,
Or whatever precious jewel there be in the heavens;
Yet there is none comparable to the Accomplished One.
In the Buddha is this precious jewel found.
On account of this truth
May there be happiness!

The tranquil Sage of the Sakyas
Realized cessation, freedom from passion,
Immortality, excellence.
There is nothing comparable to this Dhamma (teaching).
In the Dhamma is this precious jewel found.
On account of this truth
May there be happiness!

~ RATANA SUTTA, PALI TEXT

We are visitors on this planet.
We are here for ninety or one hundred years at the most.
During that period, we must try to do something good,
    something useful, with our lives.
If you contribute to other people's happiness, you will find
    the true goal, the true meaning of life.

~ HIS HOLINESS TENZIN GYATSO, THE XIV DALAI LAMA

Buddha's Discourse
on Good Will

May all beings be filled with joy and peace.
May all beings everywhere,
The strong and the weak,
The great and the small,
The mean and the powerful,

The short and the long, the subtle and the gross.
May all beings everywhere,
Seen and unseen,
Dwelling far off or nearby,
Being or waiting to become:

May all be filled with lasting joy.
Let no one deceive another,
Let no one anywhere despise another,
Let no one out of anger or resentment
Wish suffering on anyone at all.
Just as a mother with her own life
Protects her child, her only child, from harm,
So within yourself let grow
A boundless love for all creatures.

Let your love flow outward through the universe,
To its height, its depth, its broad extent,
A limitless love, without hatred or enmity.

Then as you stand or walk,
Sit or lie down,
As long as you are awake,
Strive for this with a one-pointed mind;
Your life will bring heaven to earth.

~ Sutta Nipata, Pali Text

Taoist Prayer

**Dai Temple at Mount Tai, Tai'an, Shandong Province, China,
one of the oldest and most revered Taoist shrines.**

Taoism originated in China around 2000 years ago It is a religion of unity and opposites, Yin and Yang. The world is seen as filled with complementary forces—action and non-action, light and dark, hot and cold. Taoism promotes achieving harmony or union with nature, the pursuit of a prosperous afterlife, being 'virtuous' (but not ostentatiously so) and self-development.

The Unnameable

The tao that can be told
Is not the eternal Tao.
The name that can be named
Is not the eternal Name.

The unnameable is the eternally real.
Naming is the origin of all particular things.
Free from desire, you realize the mystery.
Caught in desire, you see only the manifestations.

Yet mystery and manifestations arise from the same source.
This source is called darkness. Darkness within darkness.
The gateway to all understanding.

~ Tao Te Ching 1

Love of the Tao

Every being in the universe
Is an expression of the Tao.
It springs into existence,
Unconscious, perfect, free,
Takes on a physical body,
Lets circumstances complete it.
That is why every being
Spontaneously honors the Tao.

The Tao gives birth to all beings,
Nourishes them, maintains them,
Cares for them, comforts them, protects them,
Takes them back to itself,
Creating without possessing,
Acting without expecting,
Guiding without interfering.
That is why love of the Tao
Is in the very nature of things.

~ Tao Te Ching 51

PEACE IN THE WORLD

If there is to be peace in the world,
There must be peace in the nations.
If there is to be peace in the nations,
There must be peace in the cities.
If there is to be peace in the cities,

There must be peace between neighbors.
If there is to be peace between neighbors,
There must be peace in the home.

If there is to be peace in the home,
There must be peace in the heart.

⟿ TRADITIONAL POEM CREDITED TO LAO TZU

BE CONTENT

Fame or integrity: which is more important?
Money or happiness: which is more valuable?
Success or failure: which is more destructive?

If you look to others for fulfillment,
You will never truly be fulfilled.
If your happiness depends on money,
You will never be happy with yourself.

Be content with what you have,
Rejoice in the way things are.
When you realize there is nothing lacking,
The whole world belongs to you.

⟿ TAO TE CHING 44

INNER KNOWLEDGE

Without opening your door,
You can open your heart to the world.
Without looking out your window,
You can see the essence of all things.

～ TAO TE CHING 47

WATER

The highest good is like water.
Water give life to ten thousand things
And does not strive.

It flows in places men reject,
And so is like the Tao.

In dwelling, be close to the land.
In meditation, go deep in the heart.

In dealing with others,
Be gentle and kind.

In speech, be true.
In ruling, be just.

In business, be competent.
In action, study the timing.

There is no good in wrangling or fighting.

～ TAO TE CHING 8

Lao Tzu and the Tao Te Ching

Lao Tzu is the legendary founder of Taoism. All that is known of the life of Lao Tzu comes from sources that include fantastic stories, such attributing to him magical powers and a 400 year life span. Chinese scholars have sorted through the available material and generally agree on certain basics of Lao Tzu's life.

It is generally believed that Lao Tzu was born as Li Erh in the Ch'u province of China in the seventh century BCE. He was the curator of the Royal Library at Loyang when he became disgusted with the corruption of the royal court and left. As he was leaving the city on his westward journey into self-imposed exile, the gatekeeper stopped him and asked him to write a book of his teachings. The two volume work of short rhyming poems, called Tao Te Ching (*The Book of the Way of Virtue*) was the result.

The text is both simple and mystical, worthy of contemplation. Confucius is reputed to have said, "The dragon is beyond my knowledge; it ascends into the heaven on the cloud and the wind. Today I have seen Lao Tsu and he is like a dragon!"

Lao Tzu is an honorific title, meaning "Old Sage" given to Li Erh by his disciples. He is considered a philosopher and scholar rather than a religious leader as his writings do not mention God.

Reciting passages from the Tao Te Ching has been a spiritual practice for over 2,000 years and plays a central role in Taoist prayer pratice. For people who couldn't read and write it was an important way to learn the text, but even for those who could read, recitation was a vital expression of devotion and a way of spiritual growth.

As Taoism became institutionalized, various groups taught that recitation could do more than make the reciter a better person: the words of the Tao Te Ching were thought to have the power to cure sickness, banish evil spirits, and bring good luck.

Over time Tao Te Ching became a liturgical tool as well as a source of philosophical wisdom. Chanting Lao Tzu's ancient text became the backbone of Taoist ritual in the belief that doing so under the right conditions would prolong life and bring human beings closer to complete unity with the Tao.

The Chinese pictogram for Tao consists of two elements. On the left is the element representing a long journey. On the right is the head of a leader or priest showing his face and hat. The composite depicts the need of a sage or leader to teach the Way of Virtue.

Confucian Wisdom

Temple dedicated to Confucius in Nanjing, China.

Confucianism is often said to be a philosophy without belief in God. However, while its teachings emphasize human relationships, a divine guiding hand is assumed to be at work. He said, "I do not murmur against God, nor do I grumble against man. My studies lie low, but they reach high; and there is God—He knows me. If my doctrines are to prevail, it is so ordered of God; if they are to fail, it is so ordered of God."

In conformity with other Chinese religions, such as Taoism and Buddhism, Confucian practice incorporates ritual sacrifice.

Confucius was a contemporary of Lao Tzu who lived during the fifth and sixth centuries BCE. His precepts are written down in The *Analects* which consists of his sayings and the Menacius containing his longer discourses.

RELATIONS WITH PARENTS

A young man should serve his parents at home and be respectful to elders outside his home. (*Analects* 1.6)

When your father is alive, observe his will. When your father is dead observe his former actions. If, for three years you do not change from the ways of your father, you can be called a 'real son.' (*Analects* 1.11)

TEACHING VIRTUE BY EXAMPLE

The Master said, "I was not born with knowledge. I love what is old and am assiduous in pursuing it." (*Analect* 7.20)

The Master said, "When walking in a group of three, my teachers are always present. I draw out what is good in them so as to emulate it myself, and what is not good in them so as to alter it in myself." (*Analect* 7.22)

When the Master was at leisure, his manner was relaxed and easy. (*Analect* 7.4)

When the Master dined by the side of one who was in mourning, he never ate his fill. (Analect 7.9)

If on a certain day the Master cried, he did not on that day sing. (*Analect* 7.10)

SEEKING TRUTH

If the masses hate someone, one must investigate the case; if the masses love someone, one must investigate the case. (*Analect* 15.28)

Those who possess virtue must have teachings to impart, but a man with teachings to impart does not always possess virtue. (*Analect* 14.4)

Shinto Prayer

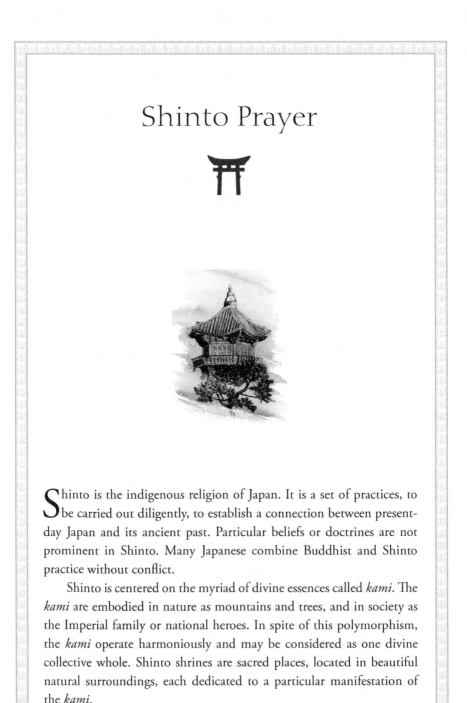

Shinto is the indigenous religion of Japan. It is a set of practices, to be carried out diligently, to establish a connection between present-day Japan and its ancient past. Particular beliefs or doctrines are not prominent in Shinto. Many Japanese combine Buddhist and Shinto practice without conflict.

Shinto is centered on the myriad of divine essences called *kami*. The *kami* are embodied in nature as mountains and trees, and in society as the Imperial family or national heroes. In spite of this polymorphism, the *kami* operate harmoniously and may be considered as one divine collective whole. Shinto shrines are sacred places, located in beautiful natural surroundings, each dedicated to a particular manifestation of the *kami*.

I Approach the Kami

Humbly, I approach the kami in prayer.
I pray to the kami of Tsubaki Grand Shrine;
Speaking with reverant heart, I present offerings and prayers. I
    come in humility and with great respect.
Kakema kumo kahikoki
Tsubaki O Kami yashiro No omae o orogami matsurite
Kashikomi kashikomi mo maosaku.

I beseech all the kami to accept these offerings
That are brought with gratitude
For the blessings and the noble teachings
That have been bestowed upon me
O kamitachi no hiroki atsuki mi megumi o katajikenami matsuri
Takaki totoki misohie no mani mani

To the divine, exalted kami, I humbly offer my prayers.
Teach me to live with a pure and sincere heart.
Grant me perserverance and that my heart be genuine,
Childlike, and true.

Grant that I stay on the path of sincerity and truth.
Grant that I be strong and diligent at my deeds.
Grant good health to my family;
Give them strength in spirit, mind, and body.
Grant that I may benefit and serve all mankind.
With awe and reverence, I humbly speak these words.

       ~ SHIN PAISHI

Shinto Offering

Divine Dwelling Mountain

The scent of the leaves of the flowering evergreen is fragrant;
Drawing near, I see countless kinsmen
Assembled all around,
Assembled all around.
On divine-dwelling mountain of sacred altar,
The leaves of the flowering evergreen have grown thick
In the presence of the kami.
Before the kami
They have grown in profusion.

∽ KAGURA-UTA

Peace for the World

I am grateful for the blessings of the kami and my ancestors And
 will practice my faith with brightness, purity and sincerity.

I will dedicate myself to serve and benefit the world
And all peoples.
I will fulfill my life mission as guided by the kami,
Dedicating myself with sincerity to achieve peace for the world
And for my nation.

From my heart, I will humbly follow and respect the kami,
Praying for harmony, prosperity,
And peace for all nations of the world.

∽ KEI SHIN SEIKATSU NO KORYO

SHINTO VIEW OF PRAYER

The purpose of Shinto prayer is the restoration of natural order and the establishment of peace under divinely constituted authority.

SACRED WORDS

The sacred liturgy shall be recited solemnly
In a great, majestic ritual,
Beseeching the kami to restore the order of nature.
When these sacred words are pronounced,
The kami of heaven will push open the heavenly gate.
Heaven's eight-fold clouds will part,
And the kami shall lend ear to the sacred words.
The kami of the earth shall climb
To the tops of the high mountains,
To the tops of the low mountains,
Dividing and sweeping away the mists of the mountains,
Restoring clarity.

∾ O Harahi No Kotoba

59

Christian Prayer

St. Peter's Basilica at Vatican

Christian prayer practices vary greatly from one church to the next. Many Christian prayers are offered extemporaneously, from the heart. Other prayers are recited verbatim.

In both ancient and modern times, Christians have made extensive use of the Old Testament Psalms. The most popular prayer revealed in the New Testament is the Our Father or Lord's Prayer. Some early Christians repeated this prayer three times a day following the pattern of Jewish prayer. The Liturgy of the Hours is composed of a series of prayers that were used in monasteries from ancient times. In its late and complete form, prayer services were held seven times during the day (Psalms 119:164) and once at midnight (Acts 16:25).

Other prayers were composed by Christian saints or church leaders of the various sects and denominations.

THE LORD'S PRAYER

Our Father, which art in heaven,
Hallowed be Thy name:
Thy kingdom come:
Thy will be done on earth as it is in heaven.
Give us this day our daily bread:
And forgive us our trespasses
As we forgive those who trespass against us.
And lead us not into temptation: but deliver us from evil.
For Thine is the kingdom
And the power and the glory, Forever.
Amen.

~ JESUS (GOSPEL OF MATTHEW)

PRAYERS FOR PEACE

Blessed are the peacemakers, for they shall be known as
the Children of God. But I say to you that hear, love your
enemies, do good to those who hate you, bless those who
curse you, pray for those who abuse you. To those that strike
you on the cheek, offer the other one also, and from those
who take away your cloak, do not withhold your coat as well.
And as you wish that others would do to you, do so to them.

~ JESUS (GOSPEL OF MATTHEW)

The Lord is My Shepherd

The Lord is my shepherd; I shall not want.
He maketh me to lie down in green pastures:
He leadeth me beside the still waters.
He restoreth my soul:
He leadeth me in the paths of righteousness for his name's sake.
Yea, though I walk through the valley of the shadow of death,
I will fear no evil:
For thou art with me;
Thy rod and thy staff they comfort me.
Thou preparest a table before me in the presence of mine enemies:
Thou anointest my head with oil;
My cup runneth over.
Surely goodness and mercy shall follow me all the days of my life: And
I will dwell in the house of the Lord for ever.

~ Psalm 23

I lift up my eyes

I lift up my eyes to the hills-where does my help come from?
My help comes from the Lord, the Maker of heaven and earth.
He will not let your foot slip—
He who watches over you will not slumber;
Indeed, he who watches over Israel will neither slumber nor sleep.
The Lord watches over you—
The Lord is your shade at your right hand.
The sun will not harm you by day, nor the moon by night.
The Lord will keep you from all harm—he will watch over your life;
The Lord will watch over your coming and going
Both now and forever evermore.

~ Psalm 121

Church of Saint-George at Lalibela, Ethiopia

BE FOR US A MOON OF JOY

May you be for us a moon of joy and happiness. Let the young become strong and the grown man maintain his strength, the pregnant woman be delivered and the woman who has given birth suckle her child. Let the stranger come to the end of his journey and those who remain at home dwell safely in their houses. Let the flocks that go to feed in the pastures return happily. May you be a moon of harvest and of calves. May you be a moon of restoration and of good health.

∾ ETHIOPIAN PRAYER

EVENING PRAYER

Lord, let the light of your glory shine upon us,
And lead us through the darkness of this world
To the radiant joy of our eternal home.
We ask this through our Lord Jesus Christ, your Son,
Who lives and reigns with you and the Holy Spirit, one God, forever
    and ever.

∾ FROM THE LITURGY OF HOURS (CATHOLIC)

Saint Basil's Cathedral, Russia

Almighty God and Creator, You are the Father of all people on the earth. Guide, I pray all the nations and their leaders in the ways of justice and peace. Protect us from the evils of injustice, prejudice, exploitation, conflict and war. Help us to put away mistrust, bitterness and hatred. Teach us to cease the storing and using of implements of war. Lead us to find justice, peace and freedom. Unite us in the making and creating of the tools of peace against ignorance, poverty, disease and oppression. Grant that we may grow in harmony and friendship as brothers and sisters created in Your image, to Your honor and praise. Amen.

⁓ ORTHODOX CHRISTIAN PRAYER BOOK

When mind and heart are united in prayer and the soul is wholly concentrated in a single desire for God, then the heart grows warm and the light of Christ begins to shine and fills the inward man with peace and joy. We should thank the Lord for everything and give ourselves up to His will; we should also offer Him all our thoughts and words, and strive to make everything serve only His good pleasure.

⁓ ST. SERAPHIM OF SAROV (RUSSIAN ORTHODOX)

DEALING WITH INJUSTICE

We offer our thanks to thee
For sending thy only Son to die for us all.
In a world divided by color bars,
How sweet a thing it is to know
That in thee we all belong to one family.

There are times when we, unprivileged people,
Weep tears that are not loud but deep,
When we think of the suffering we experience.
We come to thee, our only hope and refuge.

Help us, O God, to refuse to be embittered
Against those who handle us with harshness.
We are grateful to thee for the gift of laughter at all times.
Save us from hatred of those who oppress us.
May we follow the spirit of thy Son Jesus Christ.

~ BANTU PRAYER

Lord, make me an instrument of your peace.
Where there is hatred . . . let me sow love,
Where there is injury . . . pardon,
Where there is doubt . . . faith,
Where there is despair . . . hope,
Where there is darkness . . . light,
Where there is sadness . . . joy.
O Divine Master,
Grant that I may not so much seek
To be consoled . . . as to console,
To be understood . . . as to understand,
To be loved . . . as to love,
For it is in giving . . . that we receive,
It is in pardoning . . . that we are pardoned,
It is in dying . . . that we are born to eternal life.

~ PRAYER OF ST FRANCIS

Deep peace I breathe into you;
Oh weariness here, O ache, here!
Deep peace, a soft white dove to you;
Deep peace, a quiet rain to you;
Deep peace, an ebbing wave to you!
Deep peace, red wind of the east from you;
Deep peace, gray wind of the west to you;
Deep peace, dark wind of the north from you;
Deep peace, blue wind of the south to you!
Deep peace, pure red of the flame to you;
Deep peace, pure white of the moon to you;
Deep peace, pure green of the grass to you;
Deep peace, pure brown of the living earth to you;
Deep peace, pure gray of the dew to you;
Deep peace, pure blue of the sky to you!
Deep peace of the running wave to you,
Deep peace of the flowing air to you,
Deep peace of the quiet earth to you,
Deep peace of the sleeping stones to you,
Deep peace of the yellow shepherd to you,
Deep peace of the wandering shepherdess to you,
Deep peace of the flock of stars to you.
Deep peace of the Son of Peace to you.
Deep peace, deep peace.

~ OLD IRISH BLESSING OF PEACE

All shall be Amen and Alleluia.
We shall rest and we shall see.
We shall see and we shall know.
We shall know and we shall love.
We shall love and we shall praise.
Beyond our end which is no end.

~ SAINT AUGUSTINE

A Prayer of Fatima

Say the Rosary every day . . .
Pray, pray a lot and offer gifts for sinners . . .
I'm Our Lady of the Rosary,
Only I will be able to help you . . .
In the end my Immaculate Heart will triumph.

~ Our Lady of Fatima

How To Say The Rosary

Catholics are encouraged to say the Rosary each day. The Rosary consists of the repetition of a specific sequence of short prayers and meditations on the life of Jesus Christ and the Virgin Mary. A string of beads is used to count each prayer while praying.

1. Say the Apostles' Creed.
2. Pray the "Our Father."
3. Pray three "Hail Mary's" on next three beads.
4. Pray the "Glory Be to the Father."
5. Reflect on the mystery of Christ and Mary and pray the "Our Father" on the same bead.
6. Pray ten "Hail Mary's" on the next 10 beads.
7. Finish the sequence with the "Glory Be to the Father."

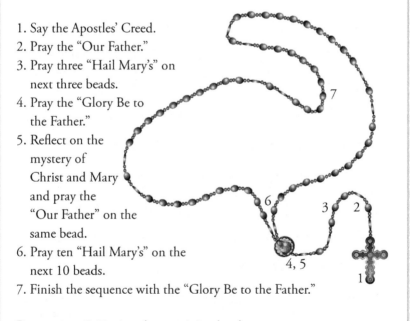

Repeat steps 5–7 using the remaining beads.

Rosary

Apostles' Creed

I believe in God, the Father Almighty, Creator of heaven and earth;
and in Jesus Christ, His only Son, our Lord: Who was conceived
by the Holy Spirit, born of the Virgin Mary; suffered under Pontius
Pilate, was crucified, died and was buried. He descended into hell; the
third day He rose again from the dead; He ascended into heaven, and
is seated at the right hand of God the Father Almighty; from thence
He shall come to judge the living and the dead. I believe in the Holy
Spirit, the Holy Catholic Church, the communion of Saints, the
forgiveness of sins, the resurrection of the body, and life everlasting.
Amen.

The Our Father:

Our Father, who art in heaven, hallowed be Thy name: Thy kingdom
come: Thy will be done on earth as it is in heaven. Give us this day
our daily bread: and forgive us our trespasses as we forgive those who
trespass against us. And lead us not into temptation: but deliver us
from evil. Amen.

The Hail Mary:

Hail Mary, full of grace; the Lord is with thee: blessed art thou among
women, and blessed is the fruit of thy womb, Jesus. Holy Mary,
Mother of God, pray for us sinners, now and at the hour of our death.
Amen

Glory Be to the Father:

Glory be to the Father, and to the Son and to the Holy Ghost.
As it was in the beginning, is now and ever shall be, world without
end. Amen.

THE GOOD SAMARITAN

From every race and land,
The victim of our day,
Abused and hurt by human hands,
Are wounded on life's way.

The priest and Levite pass
And find not time to wait.
The pressing claims of living call;
They leave them to their fate.

But one of different faith
To care he felt compelled.
His active love like Jesus' own
Uplifted, healed and held.

May this example lead,
Inspire and teach us all
That we may find in others' faith
The God on whom we call.

∼ HYMN OF THE GOOD SAMARITAN

My Heavenly Father, I thank You, through Jesus Christ,
Your beloved Son, that You have protected me, by Your grace.
Forgive, I pray, all my sins and the evil I have done. Protect
me, by Your grace, tonight. I put myself in your care, body
and soul and all that I have. Let Your holy angels be with me,
so that the evil enemy will not gain power over me. Amen.

∼ MARTIN LUTHER (LUTHERAN)

Mormon Temple, Salt Lake City.

Proclaim Peace

Therefore, renounce war and proclaim peace, and seek diligently to turn the hearts of the children to their fathers, and the hearts of the fathers to the children

And lift up an ensign of peace and make a proclamation of peace unto the ends of the earth;

And make proposals for peace unto those who have smitten you, according to the voice of the Spirit which is in you, and all things shall work together for your good.

～ Joseph Smith (Mormon)

Quaker Meetinghouse in Brighton, England

Silent Assemblies

For when I came into the silent assemblies of God's people I felt a secret power among them which touched my heart, and as I gave way unto it, I found the evil weakening in me and the good raised up.

～ Robert Barclay (Quaker)

The Joy of Prayer

Haste thee, haste thee, hour divine,
Joys ecstatic—bliss is thine.
And raptures from the throne above—
Sweeter those, than life to me,
When the world and cares do flee;
And Jesus speaks, in tones of love,
O, time of prayer! O, hour divine!—
Ecstatic joys and peace are thine!

Fairer thou than sunny rays—
Holiest time of all my days!
O, hour of love and joy, draw nigh—
Spread my faith, these eagle wings—
Speed thee where the angels sing:
Where Jesus pleads my cause on high.
O, time of prayer! O, hour divine!
Ecstatic joys and peace are thine!

Now is come the hour of prayer—
Lovely, precious Jesus, hear:
Stoop thou from thy throne above—
Bless me, bless me, Son of God!
Shed thou in my heart, abroad,
Thy saving grace, thy dying love.
O, time of prayer! O, hour divine!
Ecstatic joys and peace are thine!

O, Jesus, thou my portion art:—
Sun of my life—joy of my heart.
O, raptures! bliss—O, God of love!
Exalt my thoughts, my hopes, my soul,
Higher than where the planets roll—
Up to thy dazzling throne of love.
O, time of prayer! O, hour divine!
Ecstatic joys and peace are thine!

∽ African-American, 1837

Unitarian Universalist Society Sanctuary, near Los Angeles,
California, informally known as "the Onion."

PEACE PRAYER

Peace is flowing like a river,
Flowing out of you and me
Flowing out into the desert
Setting all the captives free.

SPIRIT OF LIFE

Spirit of Life, come unto me
Sing in my heart all the stirrings of compassion
Blow in the wind, rise in the sea
Move in the hand giving life the shape of justice
Roots hold me close, wings set me free
Spirit of life, come to me, come to me.

∼ UNITARIAN UNIVERSALIST HYMNAL

Unity Village, near Kansas City, Missouri, sponsors a Bible-based,
Christ-centered ministry that incorporates non-Christian paths to God.

THE UNIVERSAL PRESENCE

The light of God surrounds us;
The love of God enfolds us;
The power of God protects us;
The presence of God watches over us.
Wherever we are, God is.
And all is well.

~ UNITY CLOSING PRAYER FOR PROTECTION

Holy Trinity Anglican Church, Port Elizabeth, South Africa

Goodness is stronger than evil.
Love is stronger than hate.
Light is stronger than darkness.
Life is stronger than death.
Victory is ours through Him who loves us.

~ ARCHBISHOP DESMOND TUTU

Dr. Martin Luther King Memorial Prayer

Howard University (1970)

Eternal God, in the name of the Lord Jesus Christ, we would thank Thee today that Thou hast honored the purpose of our gathering. We thank Thee for sending unto us, this Nation, and the world, our great departed leader, Dr. Martin Luther King, Jr., the late possessor of unique gifts, dignity, graces, and eloquence of rare beauty. He was profoundly inspiring and challenging to his generation. The potency of his personality was marked by social progress, moral, and ethical reform.

Thou sent him to us as Thou sent Moses to Egypt to deliver the Hebrew people from slavery and bondage. We sincerely pray that the rich heritage of his philosophy may continue to inspire our Nation and Race to develop a social order of love, equality, brotherhood, compassion for black people, poor people, socially disinherited people with dignity and justice for all people.

May the torch of non-violence which he held so high continue to burn brightly in spite of the gross darkness that is covering our world today. May we never permit his dream to be an impossible dream. May we never surrender to the enemy which he fought so courageously, so bravely, and heroically to the end.

In his dwelling place among the immortals, grant that there be no future postponement, procrastination, and delay of the righteous demands that he made on the American establishment for a regeneration of our Society.

> "Minorities since time began
> Have shown the better side of man,
> And often in the list of time
> One man has made a cause sublime."

In His Name. Amen.

John Wesley's Chapel, with
statue of John Wesley in the foreground.

A Christian
View of Prayer

God's command to "pray without ceasing" is founded on the
necessity we have of his grace to preserve the life of God in
the soul, which can no more subsist one moment without it,
than the body can without air.

Whether we think of; or speak to, God, whether we act
or suffer for him, all is prayer, when we have no other object
than his love, and the desire of pleasing him.

All that a Christian does, even in eating and sleeping, is
prayer, when it is done in simplicity, according to the order of
God, without either adding to or diminishing from it by his
own choice.

Prayer continues in the desire of the heart, though the
understanding be employed on outward things.

In souls filled with love, the desire to please God is a
continual prayer.

As the furious hate which the devil bears us is termed the
roaring of a lion, so our vehement love may be termed crying
after God.

God only requires of his adult children, that their hearts
be truly purified, and that they offer him continually the
wishes and vows that naturally spring from perfect love. For
these desires, being the genuine fruits of love, are the most
perfect prayers that can spring from it.

 ∿ John Wesley (Methodist)

Jain Prayer

Shri Mahavirji Jain Temple, Rajasthan

The 15th century Jain Temple at Ranakpur, is a major pilgrimage site as it represents a culmination of Jain temple building in western India. The temple, with its distinctive domes, turrets and cupolas gives equal prominence to each of the four cardinal directions as a sign of the omnipresence of the divine in the universe.

The Jain religion emphasizes peace and respect for all living things. The Jain concept ahimsa, nonviolence, inspired the political movements of Mahatma Gandhi and Dr. Martin Luther King Jr.

UNIVERSAL FRIENDSHIP

I grant forgiveness to all living beings.
May all living beings grant me forgiveness.
My friendship is with all living beings.
I have no animosity towards any living beings.

UNIVERSAL BENEDICTION

Praise to the spiritual victors,
Praise to the liberated souls,
Praise to the spiritual leaders,
Praise to the spiritual teachers,
Praise to all saints in the world,
    who practice non-violence and
    reverence for all life in action, and
    pluralistic viewpoint in their thinking.
These five salutations are capable of destroying all the sins.
This is the first happiness among all forms of happiness.

FORGIVENESS PRAYER:

I forgive all living beings;
    may all living beings forgive me,
All living beings are my friends;
I have malice towards none.

PRAYER OF BLISS FOR ALL:

May the entire universe be blissful;
May all beings be engaged in each other's well being.
May all weakness, sickness and faults vanish;
May everyone be healthy, peaceful, and blissful everywhere.

Prayer area and the main dome of Sultan Ahmed Mosque, Istanbul, Turkey.

Islamic Prayer

Once within the doors of the mosque, every Muslim fills himself in an atmosphere of equality and love. Before their Maker they all stand shoulder to shoulder, the king along with his poorest subject, the rich arrayed in gorgeous robes with the beggar clad in rags, the white man with the black. Nay, the king or rich man standing in the back row will have to lay his head, prostrating himself before God, at the feet of a slave or a beggar standing in the front. . . . Differences of rank, wealth and color vanish.

SALAT

From the minarets of the mosques of the entire Islamic world the call to public prayer goes forth five times a day. Wherever people are, whatever they are doing, they stop, unroll prayer mats, face Mecca and recite obligatory prayers. Such prayer is called "Salat" in Arabic. The times for Salat are dawn, noon, mid-afternoon, sunset and fall of darkness.

La illaha illa Allah.
There is no God, but Allah.

In the Name of God, Most Gracious, Most Merciful,
Praise be to God, the Cherisher and Sustainer of the two worlds,
Most Gracious, Most Merciful,
Master of the Day of Judgment.
Thee do we worship
And Thine aid do we seek,
Show us the straight path,
The path of those upon whom Thou hast bestowed Thy Grace,
Those whose portion is not wrath, and who go not astray.

In the Name of God, Most Gracious, Most Merciful,
Say: He is the unique and only God,
Allah is Omnipresent, (the Eternal, the Absolute),
He begetteth not, nor is He Begotten,
And there is none like unto Him.

～ PASSAGES FROM QUR'AN 1:1–7 AND 112:1–5.
(These constitute the first part of five times daily prayer.)

CREATOR OF
HEAVEN AND EARTH

Verily your Lord is God, who created the heavens and the earth in six days, and is firmly established on the throne (of authority), regulating and governing all things. No intercessor (can plead with Him) except after His leave (hath been obtained). This is God your Lord; Him therefore serve ye: will ye not receive admonition?

To Him will be your return—of all of you.

The promise of God is true and sure. It is He Who beginneth the process of creation, and repeateth it, that He may reward with justice those who believe and work righteousness; but those who reject Him will have draughts of boiling fluids, and a penalty grievous, because they did reject Him.

It is He Who made the sun to be a shining glory and the moon to be a light (of beauty), and measured out stages for her; that ye might know the number of years and the count (of time). Nowise did God create this but in truth and righteousness. (Thus) doth He explain His Signs in detail, for those who understand.

∼ QUR'AN 10:3–5

He it is Who created the heavens and the earth in Six Days, and is moreover firmly established on the Throne (of Authority). He knows what enters within the earth and what comes forth out of it, what comes down from heaven and what mounts up to it. And He is with you wheresoever ye may be. And God sees well all that ye do.

To Him belongs the dominion of the heavens and the earth: and all affairs are referred back to God.

He merges Night into Day, and He merges Day into Night; and He has full knowledge of the secrets of (all) hearts.

Believe in God and His apostle, and spend (in charity) out of the (substance) whereof He has made you heirs. For, those of you who believe and spend (in charity),—for them is a great Reward.

∼ QUR'AN 57:4–7

Peace Be Upon
the Apostles of God

Peace and salutation to Noah among the nations!

Verily among those who followed (God's) way was Abraham. . .

He said: "I will go to my Lord! He will surely guide me!

"O my Lord! Grant me a righteous (son)!"

So We gave him the good news of a boy ready to suffer and
forbear.

Then, when (the son) reached (the age of) (serious) work with
him, he said: "O my son! I see in vision that I offer thee in
sacrifice:

Now see what is thy view!" (The son) said: "O my father! Do as
thou art commanded: thou will find me, if God so wills one
practicing Patience and Constancy!"

So when they had both submitted their wills (to God), and he had
laid him prostrate on his forehead (for sacrifice),

We called out to him "O Abraham! Thou hast already fulfilled the
vision!"

—thus indeed do We reward those who do right.

For this was obviously a trial—

And We ransomed him with a momentous sacrifice:

And We left (this blessing) for him among generations (to come)
in later times:

"Peace and salutation to Abraham!"

. . . Again (of old) We bestowed Our favour on Moses and Aaron,

And We delivered them and their people from (their) Great
Calamity;

And We helped them, so they overcame (their troubles);

And We gave them the Book which helps to make things clear;

And We guided them to the Straight Way.

And We left (this blessing) for them among generations
(to come) in later times:
"Peace and salutation to Moses and Aaron!"

. . . So also was Elijah among those sent (by Us).
Behold, he said to his people,
"Will ye not fear (God)? Will ye call upon Baal and forsake the
    Best of Creators, God, your Lord and Cherisher and the Lord
    and Cherisher of your fathers of old?"
But they rejected him, and they will certainly be called up
(for punishment),—
Except the sincere and devoted Servants of God (among them).

And We left (this blessing) for him among
generations (to come) in later times:
"Peace and salutation to such as Elijah!"
Thus indeed do We reward those who do right.
For he was one of our believing Servants.

. . . So also was Jonah among those sent (by Us).
When he ran away (like a slave from captivity) to the ship (fully)
    laden,
He (agreed to) cast lots, and he was condemned:
Then the big Fish did swallow him, and he had done acts worthy
    of blame.
Had it not been that he (repented and) glorified God,
He would certainly have remained inside the Fish till the Day of
    Resurrection.
But We cast him forth on the naked shore in a state of sickness,

. . . Glory to thy Lord, the Lord of Honour and Power!
(He is free) from what they ascribe (to Him)!
And Peace on the apostles!

∼ QUR'AN 37:79–182

A Sufi Prayer

Sufis are mystical Muslims known for their poetry,
dance and universal spirituality.

Most Gracious Lord,
Master, Messiah, and Saviour of humanity,
    We greet Thee in all humility.
Thou art the First Cause and the Last Effect,
The Divine Light and the Spirit of Guidance,
    Alpha and Omega.
Thy Light is in all forms,
Thy Love in all beings:
In a loving mother, in a kind father,
    in an innocent child, in a helpful friend,
    and in an inspiring teacher.
Allow us to recognize Thee
    in all Thy holy names and forms,
    as Rama, as Krishna, as Shiva, as Buddha,
Let us know Thee as Abraham, as Solomon,
    as Zarathustra, as Moses, as Jesus, as Mohammed,
    and in many other names and forms, known and unknown to
    the World.
We adore Thy past, Thy Presence deeply enlightens our being, and
    we look for Thy blessing in the future.
O Messenger, Christ, Nabi, the Rasul of God!
Thou whose heart constantly reacheth upwards,
Thou comest on earth with a message
    as a dove from above when Dharma decayeth, and speakest
    the Word which is put into Thy mouth as the light filleth the
    crescent moon.
Let the star of the Divine Light, shining in Thy heart be reflected
    in the hearts of Thy devotees.
May the Message of God reach far and wide,
    illuminating and making the whole humanity as one single
    brotherhood in the Fatherhood of God.
Amen.

A SUFI VIEW
OF FIVE-TIMES PRAYER

Following celestial law, the earth each day performs a complete turning. The light moves through five stages as the sun dawns, climbs to its zenith, descends downward in the slanting rays of afternoon, sets in glowing colors, and disappears into darkness. For the Sufi, this cycle is a mirror of the human life span: our dawning into the world, our growth, maturation, decline, and death. In these five stages, the soul makes its journey around another sun that never rises or sets.

The prayer invites us to awaken from the superficial self at these moments of the day. By aligning our devotional work with these natural times of power we start to move with the rhythms of God's creation in a new way, attuned to the mystical correspondences between outer and inner and to the seasons of life.

*From *The Illuminated Prayer—The Five-Times Prayers of the Sufis as revealed by Jellaludin Rumi and Bawa Muhaiyaddeen*, by Coleman Barks and Michael Green.

Sikh Prayer

The Golden Temple, officially known as the Harmandir Sahib, located in Punjab, India, was constructed in the 16th century. Visitors gather inside the temple to worship, listen to hymns, and hear the holy scripture read.

The four doors into the Harmandir Sahib symbolize the openness of Sikhs towards all people. It is intended as a place of worship for men and women from all walks of life and all religions to come and worship God equally.

The Temple is surrounded by a lake known as Amritsar, meaning "Pool of the Nectar of Immortality." The temple is a two story structure reached by a causeway known as Guru's Bridge.

The lower story is in white marble with the walls decorated with inlaid flower and animal motifs. The upper story is gold plated, crowned with a golden dome shaped like an inverted lotus. The walls within are decorated with carved wooden panels and elaborate inlay work in silver and gold. The Adi Granth, the holy scripture of Sikhism, rests on a throne beneath a jewel-encrusted canopy.

THE INDESCRIBABLE ONE

O Lord, Thou art without any form,
Symbol, caste, class or lineage.
None can describe Thy form, hue, garb, or shape.
Eternal and immutable, Resplendent in Thine own Light,
Thy Power is without limit.

Thou art the Lord of all Idras
And the King of all kings.
Sovereign of the three worlds,
Mortals, gods, demons,

Even blades of grass in the forests
Ever proclaim Thou art infinite.
Who can ever recite all Thy names!
Inspired by Thy grace,
I recite the names describing Thy deeds.

All reverence to the Eternal One,
All reverence to the Merciful One,
All reverence to the Formless One,
All reverence to the Peerless One

Having Thy domain in all quarters.
Thou art the Reveler everywhere.
Self-created, compassionate, and auspicious,
Thou art ever united with everyone.
Destroyer of bad times,
Thou art the Embodiment of Compassion.
Ever so close to everyone,
Everlasting is the treasure of Thy glory and power.

∽ JAAP SAHIB, 1–2, 199

MILLIONS OFFER STORIES

Some sing of His power-who has that power?
Some sing of His gifts, and know His sign and insignia.
Some sing of His glorious virtues, greatness and beauty.
Some sing of knowledge obtained of Him
Through difficult philosophical studies.
Some sing that He fashions the body,
And then again reduces it to dust.
Some sing that He takes life away, and then again restores it.
Some sing that He seems so very far away.
Some sing that He watches over us, face to face, ever-present.
There is no shortage of those who preach and teach.
Millions upon millions offer millions of sermons and stories.
The Great Giver keeps on giving,
While those who receive grow weary of receiving.
Throughout the ages, consumers consume . . .
O Nanak, He blossoms forth, carefree and untroubled.
True is the Master, true is His Name-speak it with infinite love.

∼ JAPJI SAHIB 2–3

CLEANSING

Whatever pleases You is the only good,
You, Eternal and Formless One.
When the hands and the feet and the body are dirty,
Water can wash away the dirt.
When the clothes are soiled and stained by urine,
Soap can wash them clean.
But when the intellect is stained and polluted by sin,
It can only be cleansed by the love of the name.
Virtue and vice do not come by mere words;
Actions repeated, over and over again, are engraved on the soul.
You shall harvest what you plant.
O Nanak, by the hukam of God's command,

We come and go in reincarnation.
Pilgrimages, austere discipline, compassion and charity
These, by themselves, bring only an iota of merit.
Listening and believing with love and humility in your mind,
Cleanse yourself with the name, at the sacred shrine deep within.

~ Japji Sahib 19–20

Guru Nanak the Founder of Sikhism

Born in 1469, near Lahore in present day Pakistan, Guru Nanak was the first of a succession of eleven Sikh Gurus. Nanak's teachings are set forth in the Guru Granth Sahib, the holy book of Sikhism. Rejecting the conflict and hostility between Hinduism and Islam, Nanak received his divine commission in a vision at age 30. "Go, rejoice of my name and teach others to do so. I have bestowed the gift of my name upon you. Let this be your calling." Thereafter he journeyed through India, Nepal, Tibet, Sri Lanka and Arabia spreading his message that the world was suffering out of hatred, fanaticism, falsehood and hypocrisy. He carried the torch of truth, heavenly love, equality, fraternity, goodness, and virtue.

Sikh View of Prayer

Sikh prayer consists largely of reading, chanting or singing from Sikh scripture. Prayers are offered three times a day, morning, evening and at bedtime with specified texts, banis, read on each occasion. When recited in the Golden Temple, the text is chanted facing the holy book. Worshippers are exhorted to recite with understanding, rather than rote repetition so as to facilitate the experience of the presence of God.

God's presence is perceived through the Guru's word:
One who thus serves the Lord feels satisfied;
He then ever dwells on the Word and is enthused.

~ Rehit Maryada, Code of Conduct, 3

Shrine of the Báb in Haifa, Israel.

Bahá'í Prayer

Bahá'í House of Worship in India

The Bahá'í Faith is the newest of worldwide religions. It was founded in Persia in 1844. Bahá'ís acknowledge the prophets of all the major religions including Abraham, Moses, Jesus, Krishna, Buddha, Muhammad, Zoroaster, the Báb and Bahá'u'lláh. Bahá'í Houses of Worship exist on every continent such as the one located in India, above. Each has nine doors built around a central sanctuary to represent diverse paths to the presence of God.

> *"Bahá'u'lláh has commanded that a place of worship be built*
> *for all the religionists of the world; that all religions, races and*
> *sects may come together within its universal shelter; that the*
> *proclamation of the oneness of mankind shall go forth from its*
> *open courts of holiness. . ."*

~ 'ABDU'L-BAHÁ

UNITY PRAYERS

O Thou kind Lord! Thou hast created all humanity from
the same stock. Thou hast decreed that all shall belong
to the same household. In Thy Holy Presence they are all
Thy servants, and all mankind are sheltered beneath Thy
Tabernacle; all have gathered together at Thy Table of Bounty;
all are illumined through the light of Thy Providence . . .

O Thou kind Lord! Unite all. Let the religions agree and
make the nations one, so that they may see each other as one
family and the whole earth as one home. May they all live
together in perfect harmony.

O God! Raise aloft the banner of the oneness of
mankind.

O God! Establish the Most Great Peace.

Cement Thou, O God, the hearts together.

O Thou kind Father, God! Gladden our hearts through
the fragrance of Thy love. Brighten our eyes through the Light
of Thy Guidance. Delight our ears with the melody of Thy
Word, and shelter us all in the Stronghold of Thy Providence.

Thou art the Mighty and Powerful, Thou art the
Forgiving and Thou art the One Who overlooketh the
shortcomings of all mankind.

~ 'Abdu'l-Bahá

. . . O Thou Provider! The dearest wish of this servant of Thy
Threshold is to behold the friends of East and West in close
embrace; to see all the members of human society gathered
with love in a single great assemblage, even as individual
drops of water collected in one mighty sea; to behold them
all as birds in one garden of roses, as pearls of one ocean, as
leaves of one tree, as rays of one sun.

Thou art the Mighty, the Powerful, and Thou art the God
of strength, the Omnipotent, the All-Seeing.

~ 'Abdu'l-Bahá

CLOSENESS TO GOD

Say: God sufficeth all things above all things, and nothing in the heavens or in the earth but God sufficeth. Verily, He is in Himself the Knower, the Sustainer, the Omnipotent.

~ THE BÁB

I created thee rich, why dost thou bring thyself down to poverty? Out of the clay of love I molded thee, how dost thou busy thyself with another? Turn thy sight unto thyself, that thou mayest find Me standing within thee, mighty, powerful and self-subsisting.

~ BAHÁ'U'LLÁH

CULTIVATING SPIRITUAL QUALITIES

. . . Let us put aside all thoughts of self; let us close our eyes to all on earth, let us neither make known our sufferings nor complain of our wrongs. Rather let us become oblivious of our own selves, and drinking down the wine of heavenly grace, let us cry out our joy, and lose ourselves in the beauty of the All-Glorious.

~ 'ABDU'L-BAHÁ

O God! Refresh and gladden my spirit. Purify my heart.
Illumine my powers. I lay all my affairs in Thy hand. Thou art my Guide and my Refuge. I will no longer be sorrowful and grieved; I will be a happy and joyful being. O God! I will no longer be full of anxiety, nor will I let trouble harass me. I will not dwell on the unpleasant things of life.
O God! Thou art more friend to me than I am to myself. I dedicate myself to Thee, O Lord.

~ BAHÁ'Í PRAYER

Prayers for Families

Glory be unto Thee, O my God! Verily, this Thy servant and this Thy maidservant have gathered under the shadow of Thy mercy and they are united through Thy favor and generosity. O Lord! Assist them in this Thy world and Thy kingdom and destine for them every good through Thy bounty and grace. O Lord! Confirm them in Thy servitude and assist them in Thy service. Suffer them to become the signs of Thy Name in Thy world and protect them through Thy bestowals which are inexhaustible in this world and the world to come. O Lord! They are supplicating the kingdom of Thy mercifulness and invoking the realm of Thy singleness. Verily, they are married in obedience to Thy command. Cause them to become the signs of harmony and unity until the end of time. Verily, Thou art the Omnipotent, the Omnipresent and the Almighty!

~ 'Abdu'l-Bahá

O my Lord, O my Lord! These two bright moons are wedded in Thy love, conjoined in servitude to Thy Holy Threshold, united in ministering to Thy Cause. Make Thou this marriage to be as threading lights of Thine abounding grace, O my Lord, the All-Merciful, the luminous rays of Thy bestowals, O Thou the Beneficent, the Ever-Giving, that there may branch out from this great tree boughs that will grow green and flourishing through the gifts that rain down from Thy clouds of grace.

Verily, Thou art the Generous. Verily, Thou art the All-Mighty. Verily, Thou art the Compassionate, the All-Merciful.

~ 'Abdu'l-Bahá

O God! Educate these children. These children are the plants of Thine orchard, the flowers of Thy meadow, the roses of Thy garden. Let Thy rain fall upon them; let the Sun of Reality shine upon them with Thy love. Let Thy breeze refresh them in order that they may be trained, grow and develop, and appear in the utmost beauty. Thou art the Giver. Thou art the Compassionate.

~ 'Abdu'l-Bahá

Bahá'í ringstone symbol representing Divine Messengers
as intermediary between heaven and earth.

BAHÁ'U'LLÁH—FOUNDER OF BAHÁ'Í FAITH

Bahá'u'lláh was born in Tehran, Persia in 1817 as Mírzá Husayn-`Alí Núrí, the son of a Minister and regional governor under the Shah. As an advocate for the poor and downtrodden, he forsook opportunities for political advancement and took up a spiritual mission under the name of Bahá'u'lláh.

On April 21, 1863, Bahá'u'lláh openly proclaimed Himself to be the Promised One of all religions in fulfillment of the universal expectations that a new messenger would come, ushering in a time of trouble followed by an era of worldwide brotherhood. He offered new wine, teachings to meet the spiritual needs of the modern age. This promise is seen by Bahá'ís to resonate with all the world's sacred books, not only the Qur'an and the Bible, but also the Hindu, Buddhist, Native American and other faith-based writings.

Bahá'u'lláh taught that humanity is one single race and that the age has come for its unification in a global society. All the world's religions are seen as coming from God. Now, as the world has become a global village, it is time for humanity to recognize its oneness and unite. "The earth is but one country and mankind its citizens." (*Tablets of Bahá'u'lláh*, 167)

His claim to divine revelation resulted in persecution and imprisonment by the Persian and Ottoman authorities. He was forced into a series of exiles in Baghdad, Constantinople, Adrianople and eventual confinement in the prison city of Akka in present day Israel. He died, while under house arrest near Akka in 1892.

Bahá'u'lláh's principal writings include the Kitáb-i-Íqán, a treatise demonstrating the unity and progressive nature of religion, the Kitáb-i-Aqdas, his book of laws for the new age, Hidden Words, a collection of wisdom proverbs and a series of letters to the kings and leaders of the earth advocating justice and international cooperation.

Prayer's Good Influence

Intone, O My servant, the verses of God
    that have been received by thee,
as intoned by them who have drawn nigh
    unto Him,
that the sweetness of thy melody
    may kindle thine own soul,
and attract the hearts of all men.
    Whoso reciteth, in the privacy of his chamber,
the verses revealed by God,
    the scattering angels of the Almighty
shall scatter abroad the fragrance
    of the words uttered by his mouth,
and shall cause the heart
    of every righteous man to throb.
Though he may, at first, remain unaware
    of its effect, yet the virtue
of the grace vouchsafed unto him
    must needs sooner or later exercise
its influence upon his soul.
    Thus have the mysteries of the Revelation
of God been decreed
    by virtue of the Will of Him
Who is the Source of power and wisdom.

                        ~ Bahá'u'lláh

'Abdu'l-Bahá

BAHÁ'Í VIEW OF PRAYER

There is nothing sweeter in the world of existence than prayer. Man must live in a state of prayer. The most blessed condition is the condition of prayer and supplication. Prayer is conversation with God. The greatest attainment or the sweetest state is none other than conversation with God. It creates spirituality, creates mindfulness, and celestial feelings, begets new attractions of the Kingdom and engenders susceptibilities of the higher intelligence.

~ 'ABDU'L-BAHÁ

Why pray?

Know thou, verily, it is becoming in a weak one to supplicate to the Strong One, and it behooveth a seeker of bounty to beseech the Glorious Bountiful One. When one supplicates to his Lord, turns to Him and seeks bounty from His Ocean, this supplication brings light to his heart, illumination to his sight, life to his soul and exaltation to his being.

During thy supplications to God and thy reciting, "Thy Name is my healing," consider how thine heart is cheered, thy soul delighted by the spirit of the love of God, and thy mind attracted to the Kingdom of God! By these attractions one's ability and capacity increase. When the vessel is enlarged the water increases, and when the thirst grows the bounty of the cloud becomes agreeable to the taste of man. This is the mystery of supplication and the wisdom of stating one's wants.

~ 'ABDU'L-BAHÁ

Oneness

"The Lord our God is one Lord."
~ JUDAISM

"But just how many Gods are there? One."
~ HINDUISM

"He is God alone: God the eternal . . .
and there is none like unto Him."
~ ISLAM

"Bear thou witness that verily He is God and
there is no God but Him, the King, the Protector,
the Incomparable, the Omnipotent."
~ BAHÁ'Í

"For us there is one God, the Father,
of whom all things are."
~ CHRISTIANITY

May fanaticism and religious bigotry be unknown, all humanity enter the bond of brotherhood, souls consort in perfect agreement, the nations of earth at last hoist the banner of truth and the religions of the world enter the divine temple of oneness, for the foundations of the heavenly religions are one reality.

~ 'ABDU'L-BAHÁ